# Faith Unfurled:
## *The Pilgrims' Quest for Freedom*
### edited by Sheila Foley

© Discovery Enterprises, Ltd.
Lowell, Massachusetts
1993

© Discovery Enterprises, Ltd., Lowell, MA 1993

ISBN 1-878668-24-2 paperback edition
Library of Congress Catalog Card Number 93-70435

10   9   8   7   6   5   4   3   2   1

*Printed in the United States of America*

*Subject Reference Guide:*
Pilgrims – New England
Mayflower Compact
Plimoth Plantation
Native Americans – Cape Cod
Pilgrims – Holland

*Credits*
Illustrated by Jeff Pollock

Reproduction of a portion of page 54
of Bradford's *Of Plymouth Plantation* of the
Mayflower Compact – Courtesy of the
State Library of Massachusetts.

*Acknowledgments*
The editor wishes to thank the following people and organizations for their help in compiling this book:

Boston Public Library
Barbara Fulton (a descendent of William Brewster)
Eleanor Hammond at the Aptucxet Trading Post
Brenda Howitson at the Massachusetts State Library
Hope Luder (teacher and historian)
Richard Pickering at Plimoth Plantation
Connie Rawson at the Stoneham Public Library

# Table of Contents

## Dedication

*This book is dedicated to seekers of freedom:*
*then, now, and in years to come.*

## Faith Unfurled
*by Sheila Foley*

In England we were made outlaws
Our district known for such
In secrecy, we worshipped there
'til thoughts turned to the Dutch

In Holland, though we knew not trades
To earn our living by
We persevered for twelve long years
When came the time to fly

No longer hidden in the dark
Our faith unfurled like sails
That blow so freely 'cross the seas
Pray God this wind prevails

# Foreword

There's more to the Pilgrims than turkey with stuffing, or a rock in Plymouth dated 1620; so much more, in fact, that the pages of this book can only begin to describe the people, their journey, and their quest for freedom.

Persecuted at home in England for their religious beliefs, the Pilgrims, then known as Separatists, left their homes with hope of a better life in Holland. Although the Dutch were tolerant of the Separatists' religion, life in Holland was still difficult.

At first the Pilgrims lived in poverty in the slums of Amsterdam. A farming people, they were ill-prepared to earn a living in this industrial city. The Dutch system of gilds and trade unions proved to be another obstacle. Men spent long years in apprenticeship programs before they could be admitted to a gild. Without that membership, it was impossible to practice a trade.

After about a year in Amsterdam, the Pilgrims moved to another Dutch city called Leyden. At first they saw no improvement in their circumstances. Still poor, still living in alleys, they somehow managed to survive and, before they left Holland, the Pilgrim congregation had become a respected part of the Leyden community.

The decision to leave their new home was not an easy one. The reasons will be discussed later, but certainly the end of Holland's twelve-year truce with Spain was a consideration. Preparation for war was a frightening prospect and the Pilgrims had no intention of being in the middle of this ongoing religious battle.

And so, the Pilgrims embarked on their most dangerous journey: west across stormy seas to the New World where their freedom was assured. Or was it?

Freedom takes many forms: freedom of religion, freedom of trade, freedom of thought to name a few. Is it possible to have too much freedom?

It seems a silly question. Of course you can never have too much freedom. But don't answer so quickly. First read the words of Governors Bradford and Winslow and letters written by Robert Cushman and Isaak DeRasiere —men who knew well the price of freedom.

Then imagine you are a native of Cape Cod in 1620, the land the Pilgrims now called their home. Did your freedom wash out with the tide that brought the Pilgrims in?

This book presents a glimpse into the lives of the Pilgrims and the native people who lived here long before their arrival. Some of the excerpts are primary sources, written by people who actually lived this part of history, and who recorded it. Although some spelling and grammar may seem different to you as you read their journals, letters and declarations, they are recorded here as they were written at the time.

You'll also be reading excerpts from historians, poets and authors who studied the Pilgrims' history and wrote about them years later. These are called secondary source materials.

## Puritans, Separatists, and the Origin of the Pilgrim Church

The Puritans were Christians who opposed certain practices of the Church of England. They thought the Established Church was overly concerned with ceremony and ritual and they wanted to get back to basics, like reading of Scripture and listening to preachers interpret the word of God. The Puritans aimed to "purify" or reform the existing church from within.

The Separatists, however, saw no hope of reform and wished only to "separate" from the Church of England so they could worship as they chose.

The Separatist Movement began in the latter part of the 16th century. During the reign of Elizabeth I, persecution of the group was not widespread although some of its leaders were imprisoned. By 1603, when James I came to the throne, it was quite a different story.

As monarch, he believed in the "divine right of kings." He declared that all his subjects must practice the religion of the Established Church. Those who refused would be forced to conform or be thrown into prison. Men, women, and children were jailed for their religious convictions.

Separatists became outlaws, forced to worship in secrecy. One such congregation in Scrooby used the manor house of William Brewster as their church. The leaders of this movement became known as the Pilgrim Fathers.

9

# The Scrooby Church and Its People

William Brewster had studied at Cambridge University
before beginning his career in the diplomatic service. He
was assistant to Secretary of State William Davison
under Queen Elizabeth I, and made several trips to the
Netherlands on Davison's behalf.

When Davison fell out of the Queen's favor, Brewster
went home to Scrooby in north Nottinghamshire. His
return was timely, as his ailing father was unable to per-
form his duties as "Master of the Postes."

The village of Scrooby lies along the Great North Road,
just north of Sherwood Forest, a convenient station on
the road between London and Scotland. Messengers
stopped at the manor house to exchange government
dispatches, partake of food and drink, or rest up before
the next leg of their journey.

William Brewster took over the office of Post-Master
after his father's death. Soon he would risk his career and
his reputation to become involved with the Separatist
cause. Because Brewster was in government service and
financially well-to-do, the Scrooby manor house escaped
detection as a haven for criminals for some time.

Richard Clyfton and John Robinson were also Cambridge University men. Clyfton had been rector of a
church in Babworth, but lost his position due to "heret-
ical views." John Robinson had also been ousted from
the Church of England.

*Scrooby Manor-House*

William Brewster took Clyfton and his family into his home after Clyfton was cast out of Babworth. Robinson became Clyfton's assistant, and the Scrooby Separatist Church was born.

A young man from Austerfield, two miles north of Scrooby, also became enthralled with the teachings of Clyfton and Robinson. William Bradford, an orphaned teenager from the border of Yorkshire, rebelled against his uncle, stealthily attending services at Scrooby manor house. Brewster soon took the youth under his wing.

It was primarily these four men who laid the foundation for the Pilgrim Movement.

In the following excerpt from William Bradford's history, *Of Plymouth Plantation*, he not only gives a stirring account of the reasons the Pilgrims left England, but also describes the difficulties they encountered in departing for Holland.

But after these things they could not long continue in any peaceable condition, but were hunted and persecuted on every side, so as their former afflictions were but as flea-bitings in comparison of these which now came upon them. For some were taken and clapped up in prison, others had their houses beset and watched night and day, and hardly escaped their hands; and the most were fain to flee and leave their houses and habitations, and the means of their livelihood.

Yet these and many other sharper things which afterward befell them, were no other than they looked for, and therefore were the better prepared to bear them by the assistance of God's grace and Spirit.

Yet seeing themselves thus molested, and that there was no hope of their continuance there, by a joint consent they resolved to go into the Low Countries, where they heard was freedom of religion for all men; as also how sundry from London and other parts of the land had been exiled and persecuted for the same cause, and were gone thither, and lived at Amsterdam and in other places of the land. So after they had continued together about a year, and kept their meetings every Sabbath in one place or other, exercising the worship of God amongst themselves, notwithstanding all the diligence and malice of their adversaries, they seeing they could no longer continue in that condition, they resolved to get over into Holland as they could. Which was in the year 1607 and 1608 . . .

Being thus constrained to leave their native soil and country, their lands and livings, and all their friends and familiar acquaintance, it was much; and thought marvelous by many. But to go into a country they knew not but by hearsay, where they must learn a new language and get their livings they knew not how, it being a dear place and subject to the miseries of war, it was by many thought an adventure almost desperate; a case intolerable and a misery worse than death. Especially seeing they were not acquainted with trades nor traffic (by which that country doth subsist) but had only been used to a plain country life and the innocent trade of husbandry. But these things did not dismay them, though they did sometimes trouble them; for their desires were set on the ways of God and to enjoy His ordinances; but they rested on His providence, and knew Whom they had believed. Yet this was not all, for though they could not stay, yet were they not suffered to go; but the ports and havens were shut against them, so as they were fain to seek secret means of conveyance, and to bribe and fee the mariners, and give extraordinary rates for their passages. And yet were they often times betrayed, many of them, and both they and their goods intercepted and surprised, and thereby put to great trouble and charge, of which I will give an instance or two and omit the rest.

There was a large company of them purposed to get passage at Boston in Lincolnshire, and for that end had hired a ship wholly to themselves and made agreement with the master to be ready at a certain day, and take them and their goods in at a convenient place, where they accordingly would all attend in readiness. So after long waiting and large expenses, though he kept not day with them, yet he came at length and took them in, in the night. But when he had them and their goods aboard, he betrayed them, having beforehand complotted with the searchers and other officers so to do; who took them, and put them into open boats, and there rifled and ransacked them, searching them to their shirts for money, yea even the women further than became modesty; and then carried them back into the town and made them a spectacle and wonder to the multitude which came flocking on all sides to behold them. Being thus first, by these catchpoll officers rifled and stripped of their money, books and much other goods, they were presented to the magistrates, and messengers sent to inform the Lords of the Council of them; and so they were committed to ward. Indeed the magistrates used them courteously and showed them what favour they could; but could not deliver them till order came from the Council table. But the issue was that after a month's imprisonment the greatest part were dismissed and sent to the places from whence they came; but seven of the principal were still kept in prison and bound over to the assizes.

The next spring after, there was another attempt made by some of these and others to get over at another place. And it so fell out that they [happened upon] a Dutchman at Hull, having a ship of his own belonging to Zealand. They made agreement with him, and acquainted him with their condition, hoping to find more faithfulness in him than in the former of their own nation; he bade them not fear, for he would do well enough. He was by appointment to take them in between Grimsby and Hull, where was a large common a good way distant from any town. Now against the prefixed time, the women and children with the goods were sent to the place in a small bark which they had hired for that end; and the men were to meet them by land. But it so fell out that they were there a day before the ship came, and the sea being rough and the women very sick, prevailed with the seamen to put into a creek hard by

14

where they lay on ground at low water. The next morning the ship came but they were fast and could not stir until about noon. In the meantime, the shipmaster, perceiving how the matter was, sent his boat to be getting the men aboard whom he saw ready, walking about the shore. But after the first boatful was got aboard and she was ready to go for more, the master espied a great company, both horse and foot, with bills and guns and other weapons, for the country was raised to take them. The Dutchman, seeing that, swore his country's oath *sacremente*, and having the wind fair, weighed his anchor, hoised sails, and away.

But the poor men which were got aboard were in great distress for their wives and children which they saw thus to be taken, and were left destitute of their helps; and themselves also, not having a cloth to shift them with, more than they had on their backs, and some scarce a penny about them, all they had being aboard the bark. It drew tears from their eyes, and anything they had they would have given to have been ashore again; but all in vain, there was no remedy, they must thus sadly part. And afterward endured a fearful storm at sea, being fourteen days or more before they arrived at their port; in seven whereof they neither saw sun, moon nor stars, and were driven near the coast of Norway; the mariners themselves often despairing of life, and once with shrieks and cries gave over all, as if the ship had been foundered in the sea and they sinking without recovery. But when man's hope and help wholly failed, the Lord's power and mercy appeared in their recovery; for the ship rose again and gave the mariners courage again to manage her. And if modesty would suffer me, I might declare with what fervent prayers they cried unto the Lord in this great distress (especially some of them) even without any great distraction. When the water ran into their mouths and ears and the mariners cried out, "We sink, we sink!" they cried (if not with miraculous, yet with a great height or degree of divine faith), "Yet Lord Thou canst save! Yet Lord Thou canst save!" with such other expressions as I will forbear. Upon which the ship did not only recover, but shortly after the violence of the storm began to abate, and the Lord filled their afflicted minds with such comforts as everyone cannot understand, and in the end brought them to their desired haven, where the people came flocking, admiring their deliverance; the storm having been so long and sore, in which much hurt had been done, as the master's friends related unto him in their congratulations.

But to return to the others where we left. The rest of the men that were in greatest danger made shift to escape away before the troop could surprise them, those only staying that best might be assistant unto the women. But pitiful it was to see the heavy case of these poor women in this distress; what weeping and crying on every side, some for their husbands that were carried away in the ship as is before related; others not knowing what should become of them and their little ones; others again melted in tears, seeing their poor little ones hanging about them, crying for fear and quaking with cold. Being thus apprehended, they were hurried from one place to another and from one justice to another, till in the end they knew not what to do with them; for to imprison so many women and innocent children for no other cause (many of them) but that they must go with their husbands, seemed to be unreasonable and all would cry out of them. And to send them home again was as difficult; for they alleged, as the truth was, they had no homes to go to, for they had either sold or otherwise disposed of their houses and livings. To be short, after they had been thus turmoiled a good while and conveyed from one constable to another, they were glad to be rid of them in the end upon any terms, for all were wearied and tired with them. Though in the meantime they (poor souls) endured misery enough; and thus in the end necessity forced a way for them.

But that I be not tedious in these things, I will omit the rest, though I might relate many other notable passages and troubles which they endured and underwent in these their wanderings and travels both at land and sea; but I haste to other things. Yet I may not omit the fruit that came hereby, for by these so public troubles in so many eminent places their cause became famous and occasioned many to look into the same, and their godly carriage and Christian behaviour was such as left a deep impression in the minds of many. And though some few shrunk at these first conflicts and sharp beginnings (as it was no marvel) yet many more came on with fresh courage and greatly animated others. And in the end, notwithstanding all these storms of opposition, they all gat over at length, some at one time and some at another, and some in one place and some in another, and met together again according to their desires, with no small rejoicing.

# Pilgrimage to Holland

Bit by bit, the Pilgrim Congregation, about 125 in all, emigrated to Holland thinking this was their final destination. They stayed in the Netherlands for "eleven or twelve years" according to Bradford. During this time, there were many marriages, births, and deaths. Some left the flock, while new converts joined their cause. Several of the Separatists even became Dutch citizens.

But the cities of Holland were overcrowded and the Pilgrims' wages low. Living conditions were far from comfortable. In 1609, even William Brewster, who had studied at Cambridge and held a government post in England, was forced to live in squalor. Dutch burial records show that a child of his died that year and that the family lived in the STINK-STEEG, meaning Stench Lane.

Their reasons for leaving Holland are discussed in the next two primary source passages.

From *The England and Holland of the Pilgrims*

Moreover, old age was stealing upon many. The danger also grew greater daily of absorption into the Dutch nation and of losing their English characteristics, to which they clung with intensest loyalty. The strain of their life was ruining not merely the happiness but even the bodily vigor of their children, and inevitable moral temptations had proved too much already for some. Nor could they bring themselves to abandon the missionary purpose which they had cherished from the first, that they might demonstrate somewhere the value to mankind of a pure and democratic church.

From *Of Plymouth Plantation*

*It may seem strange that it should seem easier to emigrate to the American wilderness than to a Dutch city; but the Netherlands were overpopulated in relation to the economic system of that day, and the standard of living in the handicrafts, the only occupations open to English immigrants, was low.*

In the following passage, the hardships of living in Holland are weighed against the anticipated dangers and problems of starting a new life in America. The Pilgrims' fear of the natives was based upon reports from the Virginia Colony.

Yea, some preferred and chose the prisons in England rather than this liberty in Holland with these afflictions. But it was thought that if a better and easier place of living could be had, it would draw many and take away these discouragements.

. . . so they like skillful and beaten soldiers were fearful either to be entrapped or surrounded by their enemies so as they should neither be able to fight nor fly. And therefore thought it better to dislodge betimes to some place of better advantage and less danger, if any such could be found. . . .

The place they had thoughts on was some of those vast and unpeopled countries of America, which are fruitful and fit for habitation, being devoid of all civil inhabitants, where there are only savage and brutish men which range up and down, little otherwise than the wild beasts of the same. This proposition being made public and coming to the scanning of all, it raised many variable opinions amongst men and caused many fears and doubts amongst themselves. . . . it was a great design and subject to many unconceivable perils and dangers; as, besides the casualties of the sea (which none can be freed from), the length of the voyage was such as the weak bodies of women and other persons worn out with age and travail (as many of them were) could never be able to endure. And yet if they should, the miseries of the land which they should be exposed unto, would be too hard to be borne and likely, some or all of them together, to consume and utterly to ruinate them. For there they should be liable to famine and nakedness and the want, in a manner, of all things. The change of air, diet and drinking of water would infect their bodies with sore sicknesses and grievous diseases. And also those which should escape or overcome these difficulties should yet be in continual danger of the savage people, who are cruel, barbarous and most treacherous, being most furious in their rage and merciless where they overcome; . . .

It was further objected that it would require greater sums of money to furnish such a voyage and to fit them with necessaries, than their consumed estates would amount to; and yet they must as well look to be seconded with supplies as presently to be transported. Also many precedents of ill success and lamentable miseries befallen others in the like designs were easy to be found . . . besides their own experience, in their former troubles and hardships in their removal into Holland, and how hard a thing it was for them to live in that strange place, though it was a neighbour country and a civil and rich commonwealth.

It was answered, that all great and honourable actions are accompanied with great difficulties and must be both enterprised and overcome with answerable courages. ...They lived here but as men in exile and in a poor condition, and as great miseries might possibly befall them in this place; for the twelve years of truce were now out and there was nothing but beating of drums and preparing for war, the events whereof are always uncertain. The Spaniard might prove as cruel as the savages of America, and the famine and pestilence as sore here as there, and their liberty less to look out for remedy.

After many other particular things answered and alleged on both sides, it was fully concluded by the major part to put this design in execution and to prosecute it by the best means they could.

# The Merchant Adventurers

After deciding to make the trip to America, there was the question of money and transportation. Who would finance the trip and how?

After several failed attempts to obtain funds, the Pilgrims were approached by Thomas Weston, a London merchant. Weston represented the Merchant Adventurers, a group which had been granted some land by the Virginia Company.

Weston's proposal was well-received by the Pilgrims. They sent two of their own men, Carver and Cushman, to London to work out details with the Adventurers. A contract was drawn up in which, in exchange for ships and supplies, the Pilgrims were to work in America for seven years for the good of the Merchant Adventurers. They were to labor five days a week for the company, having two days to themselves.

In the summer of 1620, the Leyden Congregation began selling their homes and settling finances in preparation for the trip. John Carver was sent to Southampton to arrange for supplies, while Robert Cushman dealt directly with Weston and the Merchants in London.

At the last minute, Weston changed one of the clauses in the original contract. Now the Pilgrims would have to work almost full-time for the company, amounting to what could be considered out and out slavery!

*Portrait of Edward Winslow*

The Pilgrims blamed Cushman for the blunder, but by this time they had no choice but to leave Holland. They had sold all their belongings and soon it would be autumn. If they were going, it had to be now.

Edward Winslow, later to be Governor of Plymouth Colony, joined the Pilgrim church in Leyden. His thoughts on leaving that city were given at the Farewell Feast:

From *Story of the Pilgrim Fathers*

And when the ship [the *Speedwell*] was ready to carry us away, the brethren that stayed...at Leyden feasted us that were to go, at our Pastor's house, [it] being large; where we refreshed ourselves, after our tears, with singing of *Psalms*, making joyful melody in our hearts as well as with the voice, there being many of the Congregation very expert in music; and indeed it was the sweetest melody that ever mine ears heard....

After this, they [who stayed] accompanied us to Delfshaven [*about 24 miles from Leyden*], where we were to embark; and there feasted us again.

# The Story of the *Speedwell*

From *Of Plymouth Plantation*
*So they left that goodly and pleasant city which had been their resting place near twelve years; but they knew they were pilgrims, and looked not much on those things, but lift up their eyes to the heavens, their dearest country, and quieted their spirits.*

The Pilgrims voyage to America was to be made in two ships. The *Speedwell*, the smaller ship, was sent to Delfshaven to pick up the Leyden group. The larger *Mayflower* would meet them in Southampton. William Bradford tells us why only the *Mayflower* made the journey to New England.

From *The Story of the Pilgrim Fathers*
. . .they set sail from thence [*Southampton*], about the 5th of August [1620].

Being thus put to sea, they had not gone far; but Master REYNOLDS, the Master of the lesser ship, complained that he found his ship so leak[y] as he durst not put further to sea till she was mended. So the Master of the bigger ship, called Master JONES, being consulted with; they both resolved to put into Dartmouth, and have her there searched and mended: which accordingly was done, to their great charge; and loss of time, and [of] a fair wind. She was here thoroughly searched from stem to stern. Some leaks were found and mended: and now it was conceived by the workmen and all, that she was sufficient; and [that] they might proceed without either fear or danger.

So with good hopes, from hence they put to sea again, conceiving they should go comfortably on; not looking for any more lets [*hindrances*] of this kind: but it fell out otherwise. For after they were gone to sea again, above 100 leagues without [*beyond*] Land's End; holding company together all this while: the Master of the small ship complained [that] his ship was so leaky, as he must bear up, or sink at sea; for they could scarce free her with much pumping. So they [*i.e. Captains JONES and REYNOLDS*] came to [a] consultation again; and resolved [for] both ships to bear up back again, and put into Plymouth: which accordingly was done.

But no special leak could be found; but it was judged to be the general weakness of the ship, and that she would not prove sufficient for the voyage.

Upon which, it was resolved to dismiss her, and part of the Company; and [to] proceed with the other ship. The which, though it was grievous and caused great discouragement, was put in execution. So after they had took out such provision as the other ship could well stow, and concluded what number, and what persons to send back; they made another sad parting: the one ship going back for London; and the other was to proceed on her voyage.

Those that went back [*about* 18 *or* 20] were, for the most part, such as were willing so to do; either out of some discontent, or [the] fear they conceived of the ill success of the Voyage [*Expedition*]: seeing so many crosses befallen, and the year time so far spent. But others, in regard of their own weakness [of health] and charge of many young children, were thought least useful, and most unfit to bear the brunt of this hard adventure: unto which work of GOD and judgement of their bretheren, they were contented to submit. And thus, like GIDEON's army, this small number was divided: as if the LORD, by this work of his Providence, thought these few too many for the great work he had to do.

But here, by the way, let me show, how afterwards it was found that the leakiness of this ship was partly by [her] being overmasted, and too much pressed with sails. For after she was sold, and put into her old trim; she made many voyages, and performed her service very sufficiently; to the great profit of her owners.

But more especially, by the cunning and deceit of the Master and his [ship's] company; who were hired to stay a whole year in the country: and now fancying dislike, and fearing want of victuals, they plotted this stratagem to free themselves; as afterwards was known, and by some of them confessed. For they apprehended [*thought*] that the greater ship, being of force [*better manned and armed*] and in which most of the provisions were stowed; she would retain enough for herself, whatsoever became of them or the passengers: and indeed such speeches had been cast out by some of them. And yet, besides other incouragements, the Chief of them that came from Leyden went in this ship, to give the Master content. But so strong was self love and his fears, as he forgot all duty and former kindnesses, and dealt thus falsely with them; though he pretended otherwise.

Amongst those that returned was Master CUSHMAN and his family: whose heart and courage was gone from him before, as it seems; though his body was with them till now he departed.

Robert Cushman was a passenger on the *Speedwell*. When it was determined that the smaller ship would not make the trip, he was one of those left behind. Many of the Pilgrims were still angry at his failure to keep their original contract with Weston. Here is an excerpt from a letter written by Cushman after the *Speedwell* disaster.

Our pinnace [, the *Speedwell*,] will not cease leaking; else, I think, we had been half way at Virginia. Our voyage hither hath been as full of crosses as ourselves have been of crookedness. We put in here to trim her; and I think, as others also, if we had stayed at sea but three or four hours more, she would have sunk right down. And though she was twice trimmed at [South]hampton; yet now she is as open and [as] leaky as a sieve: and there was a board, two feet long, a man might have pulled off with his fingers; where the water came in as at a mole hole.

We lay at [South]hampton seven days [30 *July*—5 *Aug.* 1620], in fair weather, waiting for her: and now we lie here waiting for her in as fair a wind as can blow, and so have done these four days [13—17 *August*]; and are like[ly] to lie four more [*they actually left on 23 August*], and by that time the wind will happily [*haply*] turn, as it did at [Sout]hampton. Our victuals will be half eaten up, I think, before we go from the coast of England;

and, if our voyage last long, we shall not have a month's victuals when we come in the country.

Near[ly] £700 hath been bestowed [*spent*] at [Sout] hampton, upon what I know not. Master [CHRISTOPHER] MARTIN saith, He neither can, nor will, give any account of it. And if he be called upon for accounts; he crieth out of unthankfulness for his pains and care, that we are suspicious of him: and flings away, and will end nothing. Also he so insulteth over our poor people [*the Leyden Pilgrims*], with such scorn and contempt, as if they were not good enough to wipe his shoes. It would break your heart to see his dealing, and the mourning of our people. They complain to me; and, alas, I can do nothing for them. If I speak to him, he flies in my face, as [if I were] mutinous; and saith, No complaints shall be heard or received but by himself: and saith, They are froward and waspish discontented people, and I do ill to hear them. There are others that would lose all they have put in, or make satisfaction for what they have had, that they might depart: but he will not hear them; nor suffer them to go ashore, lest they should run away.

# On the *Mayflower*

In early September of 1620, the *Mayflower* set sail. Captain Christopher Jones and his crew and 102 passengers weathered nine long weeks on the open Atlantic.

Only 41 of those passengers came seeking religious freedom. They called themselves saints, and the others strangers. Numbered among the strangers were John Alden, Priscilla Mullins and Myles Standish.

Many of the strangers were members of the Church of England, mainly from London or the southeast. Some had been hired by the Merchant Adventurers.

Two *Mayflower* passengers died at sea, and one child was born on the voyage—appropriately named Oceanus. Peregrine White also came into this world aboard ship, in Cape Cod (Provincetown) Harbor in December of 1620.

On November 19, 1620 land was sighted. Captain Jones was to have put in at Hudson's River in New Amsterdam. The ship had been blown off course, but the Pilgrims insisted he steer her southward. When they "fell amongst dangerous shoals and roaring breakers," according to Bradford, they decided to land at Cape Cod, which they did in safety. There they thanked the Lord for their deliverance. Elder (William) Brewster, chosen as their new spiritual leader in the absence of John Robinson, undoubtedly led his small congregation in prayer.

*The* Mayflower II, *a replica of the original* Mayflower, *is in* Plymouth Harbor.

For the Pilgrims, their great journey had ended. But it was winter, and winter has a way of putting freedom on ice. They were confined to the ship for shelter until a proper place could be found for their habitation.

But the Pilgrims were not the only inhabitants of Cape Cod, and their passage to the New World did not go unnoticed.

# *Mayflower* Passengers

## Saints

ISAAC ALLERTON, tailor
MARY ALLERTON, his wife
BARTHOLOMEW ALLERTON, their son
MARY ALLERTON, their daughter
REMEMBER ALLERTON, another daughter
WILLIAM BRADFORD, silk weaver
DOROTHY BRADFORD, his wife
WILLIAM BREWSTER, printer
MARY BREWSTER, his wife
LOVE BREWSTER, their son
WRESTLING BREWSTER, another son
JOHN CARVER, merchant
CATHERINE CARVER, his wife
FRANCIS COOKE, wool comber
JOHN COOKE, his son
JOHN CRACKSTON
JOHN CRACKSTON, his son
MOSES FLETCHER, blacksmith
SAMUEL FULLER, physician
JOHN GOODMAN, linen weaver
DESIRE MINTER, unwed girl of 20
DEGORY PRIEST, hatter
THOMAS ROGERS, merchant
JOSEPH ROGERS, his son
EDWARD TILLEY, cloth maker
ANNE TILLEY, his wife
JOHN TILLEY, silk worker
BRIDGET TILLEY, his wife
ELIZABETH TILLEY, their daughter
THOMAS TINKER, wood sawyer
————— TINKER, his wife
————— TINKER, their son
JOHN TURNER, merchant
————— TURNER, his son
————— TURNER, another son
WILLIAM WHITE, wood carver
SUSANNA WHITE, his wife
RESOLVED WHITE, their daughter
PEREGRINE WHITE, their son, born at sea
EDWARD WINSLOW, printer
ELIZABETH WINSLOW, his wife

## Servants

JOHN HOOKE
RICHARD MORE
————— MORE, his brother
ROGER WILDER
JASPER MORE
WILLIAM LATHAM
JOHN HOWLAND
WILLIAM BUTTEN, died at sea
EDWARD DOTEY
EDWARD LEISTER
JOHN LANGEMORE
ROBERT CARTER

WILLIAM HOLBECK
EDWARD THOMPSON
ELLEN MORE
ELIAS STORY
GEORGE SOULE
————— —————, an unknown maid

## Strangers

JOHN BILLINGTON
ELLEN BILLINGTON, his wife
FRANCIS BILLINGTON, their son
JOHN BILLINGTON, another son
RICHARD BRITTERIDGE
PETER BROWNE
JAMES CHILTON, tailor
————— CHILTON, his wife
MARY CHILTON, their daughter
RICHARD CLARKE
HUMILITY COOPER
FRANCIS EATON, carpenter
SARAH EATON, his wife
SAMUEL EATON, their son
EDWARD FULLER
ANN FULLER, his wife
SAMUEL FULLER, their son
RICHARD GARDINER
STEPHEN HOPKINS, merchant
ELIZABETH HOPKINS, his wife
GILES HOPKINS, their son
CONSTANCE HOPKINS,
    their daughter
DAMARIS HOPKINS, another son
OCEANUS HOPKINS, born at sea
EDMUND MARGESON
CHRISTOPHER MARTIN, died at sea
————— MARTIN, his wife
SOLOMON PROWER, Martin's stepson
WILLIAM MULLINS, shopkeeper
ALICE MULLINS, his wife
PRISCILLA MULLINS, their daughter
JOSEPH MULLINS, their son
JOHN RIGDALE
ALICE RIGDALE, his wife
HENRY SAMSON
MYLES STANDISH, soldier
ROSE STANDISH, his wife
RICHARD WARREN, merchant
THOMAS WILLIAMS
GILBERT WINSLOW,
    brother of Edward

## Hired Hands

JOHN ALDEN, cooper
JOHN ALLERTON, mariner
————— ELLIS, sailor
THOMAS ENGLISH, mariner
WILLIAM TREVORE, sailor

# Plymouth Bay Map 1620-1650

The lower left area of this map shows the Billington Sea.

# The Indian Viewpoint

The following passage from William Martin's fictional work *Cape Cod* may just describe what the native people thought as they watched the *Mayflower* skirt their shores.

From *Cape Cod* (iii)

More had come.

Men in a great canoe, as big as a hillside, driven by white wings on the wind. Men whose faces grew hair like the pelt of the beaver. Men who dressed in layers of colored skins, yet whose own skin was as white as birchbark. Men who brought some good things...and many bad.

The canoe, called a ship, was the largest that Autumnsquam had ever seen, and he felt fear, like the taste of blood, rise in his throat.

He had been a boy when *les francaises* appeared in the Bay of the Nausets, fifteen summers before. He still remembered the one called Champlain, who sat on the bow of his canoe and made pictures of the land.

The next year *les francaises* had visited the Nausets again, then sailed south to the land of the Monomoyicks. They stayed too long and would not leave, and there was a fight in which many whites and Monomoyicks died.

More came after that. Some flew the red-crossed flag of the English, others the flowered flag of *les francaises*.

A few showed a black flag with a white skull and bones. Some simply fished. Some traded knives and metal for pelts. A few pretended trade only to steal Nausets for slaves, and their evil stained every white.

But in the life of the Nausets and the Wampanoag nation, in the sachemdoms from the tip of the Narrow Land to the edge of the Narragansett Bay, the Great Sickness that followed the white men would be remembered before anything else, good or bad.

It began, they said, to the north, in the Penobscot Land, where the whites fished and traded. It reached Autumnsquam's village shortly after a runner brought news of it. An old man began to shiver and felt great pains in his head. His skin grew hot as a baking stone. His woman bathed him in cold water, and the *pauwau* sang his song. It did no good. The old man died four days later.

But few noticed, because by then, people everywhere were shivering and growing hot at the same time. Little children went so mad with the heat inside their heads that they did not know their own parents. Brave men who had hunted wolves whimpered like old women with pain. Some jumped into the sea to cool their misery, and some of them drowned.

But few noticed, because Wampanoags were dying everywhere. Autumnsquam did not notice, because he was burying his baby daughter and his own woman.

The dying began in fall and did not end until spring. In some parts of the Wampanoag nation, there were more dead than alive, more dead than the living could bury, and the bones lay bleaching on the sand. For reasons that no man knew, there was less dying on the

*Drawing of Wampanoag Indians recreating the daily activities of their ancestors at the Plimoth Plantation.*

Narrow Land than in other places, but still there was too much.

Before the white man, there had never been such sickness, the Nausets had never before been dragged into slavery, and the eastern horizon had been the home of the dawn, not the lair of great canoes called ships. Now, the Nausets were no longer friendly to the whites. They enslaved those who were shipwrecked and drove off those who came to trade. But this was the biggest ship that ever had come.

And it was turning south.

Autumnsquam feared that they were searching for the Bay of the Nausets, to steal more of his people and punish them for what they had done to other whites. He would bring the warning, and his people would be ready.

He had learned from his father to measure his gait by the movement of the copper pendants that hung from his ears. If they bounced against his cheeks, it meant that he was running too fast. If they made no motion, he went like the turtle. But if he kept a strong, steady pace, he would feel them swing in rhythm with his gait, and he would go fast yet with dignity.

Because there were fewer now to use the path, much thicket had grown over it, but Autumnsquam was young and strong and wore his winter breeches, and what he could not step over, he went through. For much of the morning, the path took him along the bluff, so that he could watch the white men's ship and keep himself ahead of it.

Then the bluff gave way to long spits of sand that protected the Bay of the Nausets. The path turned inland along the shore, and Autumnsquam could no longer see the ship. This worried him some, but he kept his copper pendants swinging steadily, stopped only for a handful of pemmican, and soon smelled the cookfires of his village.

At word of the ship, the men took their bows and went to the shore. The women took the children and hid in the forest. And the Nausets waited the day through. But the white men did not come.

Then the setting sun burned through the clouds, sending long rays, like arrows, across the world. The sandspit that formed the eastern shore of their bay glimmered in the golden light. Then the arrows of sun struck something else. At first, Autumnsquam could not tell what it was, this thing that seemed to glide along the rim of the dunes. He was taken by the beauty of it and wondered if it was some new god, come to save them from the white men. Then he knew. It *was* the white men. Their ship was beyond the spit, with only its wings showing above the sand. It had gone south and was now turning north. The white men were looking for a place to land.

# The Mayflower Compact

Because the Pilgrims had landed north of where the Merchant Adventurers patent applied, there was talk that some passengers had intentions of ignoring the contract with Weston. After all, the Virginia Company had no land grants on Cape Cod. Why labor for the company when they could work for themselves and reap all the profits? This was America. There were no laws to keep the saints and the strangers together as one people. Once they got off the ship, it could be every man for himself. The lure of freedom was strong, yet wisdom prevailed.

Some of their number saw the need for a written agreement. On November 21, 1620, they gathered in the cabin of the *Mayflower* to draw up the Mayflower Compact. It bound saints and strangers alike into one "civil body politick," in other words, a government of the people, by the people, for the people.

Forty-one of the men signed their names to the historic document. Women were not allowed to sign, and most of the others were considered too young. Page 54 of Governor Bradford's "History" shows the Compact written in his own hand. This is not the original Compact (its whereabouts is unknown) but Bradford's recollection of it.

seto by them done (this their condition considered) might
be as firme as any patent; and in some respects more sure.
The forme was as followeth.

In ÿ name of god Amen. We whose names are underwriten,
the loyall subiects of our dread soueraigne Lord King Iames,
by ÿ grace of god, of great Britaine, franc, & Ireland king,
defender of ÿ faith, &c.

Haueing undertaken, for ÿ glorie of god, and aduancements
of ÿ christian faith, and honour of our king & countrie, a voyage to
plant ÿ first colonie in ÿ Northerne parts of Virginia. doe
by these presents solemnly & mutualy in ÿ presence of god, and
one of another, Couenant, & combine our selues togeather into a
ciuill body politick; for ÿ our beter ordering, & preseruation & fur=
therance of ÿ ends aforesaid; and by vertue hearof to Enacte,
constitute, and frame shuch just & equall lawes, ordinances,
Acts, constitutions, & offices, from time to time, as shall be thought
most meete & conuenient for ÿ generall good of ÿ colonie: unto
which we promise all due submission and obedience. In witnes
wherof we haue hereunder subscribed our names at Cap=
Codd ÿ .11. of Nouember, in ÿ year of ÿ raigne of our soueraigne
Lord king Iames of England, france, & Ireland ÿ eighteenth
and of Scotland ÿ fiftie fourth. An°: Dom: 1620.

After this they chose, or rather confirmed mr John caruer (a man
godly & well aproued amongst them) their gouernour for that
year. And after they had prouided a place for their goods, or
comone Store, (which were long in unlading, for mant of boats,
foulnes of ÿ winter weather, and sicknes of diuerse) and begane
some small cottages for their habitation; as time would admite
they mete and consulted of lawes, & ordors, both for their
ciuill & military gouernmente, as ÿ necessitie of their condi=
tion did require, still adding thervnto as urgent occasion
in seuerall times, and ÿ cases did require.

In these hard & dificulte beginings they found some discontents
& murmurings amongst some, and mutinous speeches & cariag
in other; but they were soone queled, & ouercome, by ÿ wis=
dome, patience, and iust & equall carrage of things, by ÿ gou:
and better part wch claue faithfully togeather in ÿ maine.
But that which was most sadd, & lamentable, was, that in 2.
or .3. moneths time halfe of their company dyed, espetialy
in Ian: & february, being ÿ depth of winter, and wanting
houses & other comforts; being Infected with ÿ scuruie &

# The Mayflower Compact

In y$^e$ name of God, Amen. We whose names are underwriten, the loyall subjects of our dread soveraigne Lord, King James, by y$^e$ grace of God, of Great Britaine, Franc, & Ireland king, defender of y$^e$ faith, &c., haveing undertaken, for y$^e$ glorie of God, and advancemente of y$^e$ Christian faith, and honour of our king & countrie, a voyage to plant y$^e$ first colonie in y$^e$ Northerne parts of Virginia, doe by these presents solemnly & mutualy in y$^e$ presence of God, and one of another, covenant & combine our selves togeather into a civill body politick, for our better ordering & preservation & furtherance of y$^e$ ends aforesaid; and by vertue hearof to enacte, constitute, and frame such just & equall lawes, ordinances, acts, constitutions, & offices, from time to time, as shall be thought most meete & convenient for y$^e$ generall good of y$^e$ Colonie, unto which we promise all due submission and obedience. In witnes wherof we have hereunder subscribed our names at Cap-Codd y$^e$ 11. of November, in y$^e$ year of y$^e$ raigne of our soveraigne lord, King James, of England, France, & Ireland y$^e$ eighteenth, and of Scotland y$^e$ fiftie fourth. An$^{\circ}$: Dom. 1620.

*Note:* Keep in mind that old style and new style calendars differ. In the case of the Mayflower Compact there was a 10 day discrepancy. See reference to date of Compact on page 39.

# Dorothy Bradford's Letter to Her Son
*Historical Fiction by Sheila Foley*

Dear John,

I know not when this letter may reach you. Our ship cannot return to England as it remains our only shelter in this harsh country. Perhaps you will be old enough to understand when this post arrives at Leyden.

By God's mercy we have safe arrived in the northern parts of Virginia, having landed at the place called Cape Cod. The winter season sets itself against us as we intrude upon its loneliness. I am lonely as well.

I miss you mightily, but the course of our journey was not kind, and one so young best not be subjected to the whims of sea and sky. On our crossing, God took from us two men, and one child was born aboard this ship.

Our lives surge forth like the crest of a wave that later pulls us under as its waters abate. For me the crests come fewer and fewer. I wonder should I step upon solid earth again.

Your father is well. He is off once more with Captain Standish and other men of the company, on a voyage of exploration. They search for our place of habitation which we needs find soon.

Master Jones, captain of this ship, talks of leaving us if a site for our plantation is not found in timely fashion. He is not a cruel man but perhaps an impatient one. We pray for his deliverance as well as our own.

Elder Brewster is a comfort when fear grips the soul. His wisdom and knowledge of Scripture doth console the weak amongst us. Of these I number myself.

I know to seek my strength in the Lord, but I may not be a worthy seeker. If we should never meet again on this earth, my beloved, I pray you shall grow in the Lord's sight. Keep His faith and forever follow His path, in whatever place He deems suitable.

Your loving mother,
Dorothy Bradford

Dorothy May was sixteen years old in 1613, when she married William Bradford in Leyden. He was twenty-three. When they left for England in the *Speedwell*, their infant son, John, was left behind. In November of 1620, as passengers on the *Mayflower*, they sighted Cape Cod.

The ship anchored at what is now Provincetown on November 21. Soon small parties of men set out to explore the area, looking for the best place to settle permanently.

William Bradford was on the third such mission. It was this group that first encountered Indians and eventually decided upon Plymouth, then called Patuxet, as the site for their plantation.

On December 17, 1620, while her husband was on his voyage of exploration, Dorothy Bradford drowned in Cape Cod Harbor. Apparently she had fallen overboard while the *Mayflower* was at anchor. Bradford learned of her death upon his return on December 22. Their son John made his crossing to Plymouth in 1627.

In 1621, William Bradford became governor of Plymouth Colony. He remarried in 1623 and had four children by his second wife, Alice Southworth.

# The Billington Boys: Disaster and Discovery

Although infant John Bradford did not make the journey to New England with his parents, there were other children on the *Mayflower*. Two boys are of particular interest.

John and Francis Billington were the sons of John Billington (the following passage from Winslow and Bradford's journal calls the father Francis, but most other primary sources as well as the *Mayflower* passenger list name him John). John, the father, was known to be a troublesome sort. He was not part of the Pilgrim Congregation, but somehow joined the saints in England. He was also the first of the new colony to be punished for his offenses. Sentenced "to have his neck and heels tied together," Billington soon became remorseful and was set free.

His sons were equally mischievous and seeking their own kind of freedom, as these excerpts show.

Excerpt from Bradford and Winslow's Journal, published in *Chronicles of the Pilgrim Fathers*

"Dec. 5

The 5th day we, through God's mercy, escaped a great danger by the foolishness of a boy, one of Francis Billington's sons, who, in his father's absence, had got gunpowder, and had shot off a piece or two, and made squibs; and there being a fowling-piece charged in his father's cabin, shot her off in the cabin; there being a little barrel of powder half full, scattered in and about the cabin, the fire being within four foot of the bed between decks, and many flints and iron things about the cabin, and many people about the fire; and yet, by God's mercy no harm done."

"Jan. 8, 1621

This day Francis Billington, having the week before seen from the top of a tree on a high hill a great sea, as he thought, went with one of the master's mates to see it. They went three miles and then came to a great water, divided into two great lakes; the bigger of them five or six miles in circuit, and in it an isle of a cable length square; the other three miles in compass, in their estimation. They are fine fresh water, full of fish and fowl. A brook issues from it; it will be an excellent place for us in time."

Indeed it was an excellent source of water and fish. It became known as the Billington Sea, a name it bears today.

# Indian Relations

Squanto is a name with which we are all familiar. But who was he? It seems he was the last of the Patuxet Indians. He had been tricked aboard a ship by one Captain Hunt who kidnapped him. Squanto spent time in England before managing to get passage back to his native land. On his return, he was to find himself the last of his tribe, the rest wiped out by a plague. Luckily for the Pilgrims, he spoke English, and served as their interpreter and friend.

William Bradford gave this description of a meeting with Indians:

From *Of Plymouth Plantation*

All this while the Indians came skulking about them, and would sometimes show themselves aloof off, but when any approached near them, they would run away; and once they stole away their tools where they had been at work and were gone to dinner. But about the 16th of March, a certain Indian came boldly amongst them and spoke to them in broken English, which they could well understand but marveled at it. At length they understood by discourse with him, that he was not of these parts, but belonged to the eastern parts where some English ships came to fish, with whom he was acquainted and could name sundry of them by their names, amongst whom he had got his language. He became profitable to them in acquainting them with many things concerning the state of the country in the east parts where he lived, which was afterwards profitable unto them; as also of the people here, of their names, number and strength, of their situation and distance from this place, and who was chief amongst them. His name was Samoset. He told them also of another Indian whose name was Squanto, a native of this place, who had been in England and could speak better English than himself.

Being, after some time of entertainment and gifts dismissed, a while after he came again, and five more with him, and they brought again all the tools that were stolen away before, and made way for the coming of their great Sachem, called Massasoit. Who, about four or five days after, came with the chief of his friends and other attendance, with the aforesaid Squanto. With whom, after friendly entertainment and some gifts given him, they made a peace with him (which hath now continued this 24 years) in these terms:

1. That neither he nor any of his should injure or do hurt to any of their people.
2. That if any of his did hurt to any of theirs, he should send the offender, that they might punish him.
3. That if anything were taken away from any of theirs, he should cause it to be restored; and they should do the like to his.
4. If any did unjustly war against him, they would aid him; if any did war against them, he should aid them.
5. He should send to his neighbours confederates to certify them of this, that they might not wrong them, but might be likewise comprised in the conditions of peace.

6. That when their men came to them, they should leave their bows and arrows behind them.

After these things he returned to his place called Sowams, some 40 miles from this place, but Squanto continued with them and was their interpreter and was a special instrument sent of God for their good beyond their expectation. He directed them how to set their corn, where to take fish, and to procure other commodities, and was also their pilot to bring them to unknown places for their profit, and never left them till he died.

The following is a note from Captain Dermer:

I will first begin (saith he) with that place from whence Squanto or Tisquantum, was taken away; which in Captain Smith's map is called Plymouth; and I would that Plymouth had the like commodities. I would that the first plantation might here be seated, if there come to the number of 50 persons, or upward. Otherwise, Charlton, because there the savages are less to be feared. The Pocanockets, which live to the west of Plymouth, bear an inveterate malice to the English, and are of more strength than all the savages from thence to Penobscot. Their desire of revenge was occasioned by an Englishman, who having many of them on board, made a greater slaughter with their murderers and small shot when as (they say) they offered no injury on their parts. Whether they were English or no it may be doubted; yet they believe they were, for the French have so possessed them.

# The Voyage to Nauset

John Billington, the son, was probably upset that his brother had discovered a "great sea," so he set out on his own to explore. Unfortunately, he got lost and a search party went to find him.

From Bradford and Winslow's Journal, published in *Chronicles of the Pilgrim Fathers*

The 11th of June we set forth, the weather being very fair. But ere we had been long at sea, there arose a storm of wind and rain, with much lightning and thunder, insomuch that a spout arose not far from us. But God be praised, it dured not long, and we put in that night for harbour at a placed called Cummaquid, where we had some hope to find the boy. Two savages were in the boat with us. The one Tisquantum, our interpreter; the other Tokamahamon, a special friend. It being night before we came in, we anchored in the midst of the bay, where we were dry at a low water. In the morning we espied savages seeking lobsters, and sent our two interpreters to speak with them, the channel being between them; where they told them what we were, and for what we were come, willing them not at all to fear us, for we would not hurt them. Their answer was that the boy was well, but he was at Nauset, yet since we were there, they desired us to come ashore, and eat with them; which as soon as our boat floated, we did, and went six ashore, having four pledges for them in the boat. They brought us to their sachim, or governor, whom they call Iyanough, a man not exceeding twenty-six years of age, but very personable, gentle, courteous, and fair conditioned, indeed not like a savage, save for his attire. . . .

One thing was very grievous unto us at this place. There was an old woman, whom we judged to be no less than a hundred years old, which came to see us, because she never saw English; yet could not behold us without breaking forth into great passion, weeping and crying excessively. We demanding the reason of it, they told us she had three sons, who, when Master Hunt was in these parts, went aboard his ship to trade with him, and he carried them captives into Spain (for Tisquantum at that time was carried away also,) by which means she was deprived of the comfort of her children in her old age. We told them we were sorry that any Englishman should give them that offence, that Hunt was a bad man, and that all the English that heard of it condemned him for the same; but for us, we would not offer them any such injury, though it would gain us all the skins in the country. So we gave her some small trifles, which somewhat appeased her. After dinner we took a boat for Nauset, Iyanough and two of his men accompanying us. Ere we came to Nauset, the day and tide were almost spent, insomuch as we could not go in with our shallop; but the sachim or governor of Cummaquid went ashore, and his men with him. We also sent Tisquantum to tell Aspinet, the sachim of Nauset, wherefore we came. The savages here came very thick amongst us, and were earnest with us to bring in our boat. But we neither well could, nor yet desired to do it, because we had less cause to trust them, being they only had formerly made an assault upon us in the same place, in the time of our winter discovery for habitation. And indeed it was no marvel they did so; for howsoever, through snow or otherwise, we saw no houses, yet we were in the midst of them.

When our boat was aground, they came very thick; but we stood therein upon our ground, not suffering any to enter except two, the one being of Manomoick and one of those whose corn we had formerly found. We promised him restitution, and desired him either to come to Patuxet for satisfaction, or else we would bring them so much corn again. He promised to come. We used him very kindly for the present. Some few skins we gat there, but not many.

After sunset, Aspinet came with a great train, and brought the boy with him, one bearing him through the water, he had not less than a hundred with him; the half whereof came to the shallop side unarmed with him; the other stood with their bows and arrows. There he delivered us the boy, behung with beads, and made peace with us; we bestowing a knife on him, and likewise on another that first entertained the boy and brought him thither. So they departed from us.

# Weston and Wessagusset

In April of 1621, the *Mayflower* left Plymouth on her return to England. When the ship arrived at port, Thomas Weston, who'd helped finance the trip was upset that the ship was not laden with skins and other supplies. In his mind, the Pilgrims had ample time to show a profit and he wanted evidence of that profit himself. Little did he know that a great sickness had come amongst them and according to Bradford, "But it pleased God to visit us then with death daily, and with so general a disease that the living were scarce able to bury the dead, and the well not in any measure sufficient to tend the sick."

In the summer of 1622, two ships of Weston's came to Cape Cod. The passengers were all men: men intent on making money and taking what they could get from the land and its people.

The Pilgrims received them and offered them food and shelter until they could fend for themselves. They responded with dishonesty. In a letter Robert Cushman writes, "They are no men for us, and I fear they will hardly deal so well with the savages as they should. I pray you therefore signify to Squanto that they are a distinct body from us, and we have nothing to do with them, nor must be blamed for their faults, much less can warrant their fidelity."

It is not surprising that Weston's colony in Wessagusset, now Weymouth, caused a disturbance in the peace the Pilgrims had thus far enjoyed with the Indians.

From *Three Visitors to Early Plymouth*

...for in the Massachusetts there was a colony—I may rather say a company of idle persons, for they had no civil government among themselves, much less were able to govern and rule Indians by them. And this plantation was begun about one year and one half since by one Mr. Weston, who came this year to his plantation. But by many notorious deeds among themselves, and also having in their necessity stolen corn from the Indians, the Indians began to condemn them and would have killed all the English, but they feared that when the English of Patuxet did hear what they had done, then they would set upon the squaw sachem in the Massachusetts and so kill all the Indians in the Massachusetts. Whereupon they determined another resolution: to cut the English at Patuxet, whom they stand in fear of now, and the English at Massachusetts both at one time. But in the mean time, the great Massasoit sent to Patuxet for some physic, because he was fallen sick, and so, by God's help, he was cured. And upon his recovery, he made known the plot of the Indians of Massachusetts against us, and told us that if we would not go fight with them, he would. So at the return of our surgeon from Massasoit, came a messenger from Mr. Weston's plantation at Massachusetts, telling us that there was a plot against us by the Indians of Massachusetts. Whereupon the Governor, Mr. William

Bradford (well worthy the place), sent Captain Standish with some six or seven others to the Massachusetts to bring away the head of him that made the broil. And so, by God's goodness, he killed our chief enemy and five or six others without any hurt to our part, and brought away the head of the chiefest of them. And [it] is set on the top of our fort, and instead of an ancient, we have a piece of linen cloth dyed in the same Indian's blood, which was hung out upon the fort when Massasoit was here. And now the Indians are most of them fled from us, but they now seek to us to make peace.

The above incident prompted a letter from John Robinson, the Pilgrim's pastor in Leyden, in which he writes "Concerning the killing of those poor Indians, of which we heard at first by report, and since by more certain relation. Oh, how happy a thing had it been, if you had converted some before you had killed any! Besides, where blood is once begun to be shed, it is seldom staunched of a long time after. You will say they deserved it. I grant it; but upon what provocations and invitements by those heathenish Christians?"

# The First Thanksgiving

Americans tend to think of the Pilgrims once a year, at Thanksgiving. Although it is true that they feasted with Indians and thanked God for their health and harvest, it merits a mere paragraph in Bradford's history *Of Plymouth Plantation.*

. . . They began now to gather in the small harvest they had, and to fit up their houses and dwellings against winter, being all well recovered in health and strength and had all things in good plenty. For as some were thus employed in affairs abroad, others were exercised in fishing, about cod and bass and other fish, of which they took good store, of which every family had their portion. All the summer there was no want; and now began to come in store of fowl, as winter approached, of which this place did abound when they came first (but afterward decreased by degrees). And besides waterfowl there was great store of wild turkeys, of which they took many, besides venison, etc. Besides they had about a peck a meal a week to a person, or now since harvest, Indian corn to that proportion. Which made many afterwards write so largely of their plenty here to their friends in England, which were not feigned but true reports. . . .

# Freedom of Trade

In 1626, the Pilgrims, still in debt on their original contract and seeing no end in sight, agreed to buy out the interests of the Merchant Adventurers. Isaac Allerton served as their representative to the company.

Eight of the Pilgrim leaders, including Allerton, Bradford and Standish, assumed responsibility for working off the debt in six years' time. By starting the first commercial venture in English-speaking North America, they managed to set the Pilgrim flock free.

Their enterprise, the Aptucxet Trading Post, was built in 1627. Its location was perfect for trading with the New Amsterdam Dutch as well as nearby Indian populations.

Local currency, called wampum (also known as sewan) was the medium of exchange. Wampum was made from polished bits of shells, and had long been used by the Indians.

The Dutch knew that Aptucxet would be a success, and soon worried about a Pilgrim trade monopoly. A letter from Isaac DeRasiere, secretary to Governor Peter Minuit of Manhattan, tells all.

From *Three Visitors*

...Coming out of the river Nassau, you sail east-and-by-north about fourteen leagues, along the coast, a half league from the shore, and you then come to

"Frenchman's Point" at a small river where those of Patuxet have a house made of hewn oak planks, called Aptucxet, where they keep two men, winter and summer, in order to maintain the trade and possession. Here also they have built a shallop, in order to go and look after the trade in sewan, in Sloup's Bay and thereabouts, because they are afraid to pass Cape Malabar, and in order to avoid the length of the way; which I have prevented for this year by selling them fifty fathoms of sewans, because the seeking after sewan by them is prejudicial to us, inasmuch as they would, by so doing, discover the trade in furs; which if they were to find out, it would be a great trouble for us to maintain, for they already dare to threaten that if we will not leave off dealing with that people, they will be obliged to use other means. If they do that now, while they are yet ignorant how the case stands, what will they do when they do get a notion of it?...

## Closing Thoughts

Through introductory words and primary source material, we have tried briefly to tell the story of the Pilgrims. Where did they come from? What drove them to wander and finally settle in New England? How did they survive? And who were they, really?

More than a mismatched collection of saints and strangers, they were ordinary people who dared to be extraordinary, who dared to live what they believed.

We owe them our basic form of government, our system of free enterprise, and so many of the other freedoms that we Americans take for granted. The story of the Pilgrims is the story of America itself.

> From my years young in days of Youth,
> God did make known to me his Truth,
> And called me from my Native place
> For to enjoy the Means of Grace.
> In Wilderness he did me guide,
> And in strange lands for me provide,
> In Fears and Wants, through Weal and Woe,
> As Pilgrim passed I to and fro:...

Excerpt from William Bradford

# Definitions

*aloof* – at a distance but within view

*assize* – a judicial inquest or the verdict of the jurors.
  Plural: *assizes* - one of periodic court sessions held in
  criminal and civil cases in England or Wales

*durst* – past tense of dare (Archaic)

*froward* – obstinate, stubborn, disobedient

*pemmican* – a food prepared by North American Indians
  from lean, dried strips of meat pounded into paste,
  mixed with fat and berries, and pressed into small cakes

*sachem* – the chief of a tribe or confederation among
  some North American Indians; Narragansets used the
  word "sachim"

*shallop [shalloop]* – an open boat fitted with oars, sails,
  or both

*victuals* – food supplies

*waspish* – easily irritated or annoyed, like a wasp

# Bibliography

## Primary Sources

Arber, Edward, ed., *An English Garner, Vol. II, Ingatherings from Our History and Literature*, Southgate, London, 1879.

——————— *The Story of the Pilgrim Fathers 1606-1623 A. D.*, Ward & Downey Ltd., 1897 (more recently published by Houghton Mifflin & Co.).

Bradford, William, *Of Plymouth Plantation*, @ S.E. Morison 1952, Alfred A. Knopf, 1966.

Dexter, Henry M. and Morton, *The England and Holland of the Pilgrims*, Houghton Mifflin, 1905.

Morton, Nathaniel, *New England's Memoriall (1669)*, ed. by Hall, Howard J., Scholars Facsimiles & Reprints, N.Y., 1937.

Morton, Thomas, *New English Canaan or New Canaan*, Arno Press, a New York Times Company, 1972.

Pope, Charles Henry, ed., *The Plymouth Scrapbook*, C. E. Goodspeed & Co., 1918.

Pory, Altham, and DeRasieres, *Three Visitors to Early Plymouth*, James, Sydney V., Jr., ed., Plimoth Plantation, 1963.

Young, Alexander, ed., *Chronicles of the Pilgrim Fathers*, Freedman & Bolles, 1841.

## Other References

Archer, Gleason, *Mayflower Heroes*, The Century Company, 1931.

Hamilton, Charles, ed., *Cry of the Thunderbird: The American Indians' Own Story*, University of Oklahoma Press, 1950, reprint 1972.

Martin, William, *Cape Cod*, Warner Books, Inc., 1991.

Stoddard, Francis R., *The Truth About the Pilgrims*, General Society of Mayflower Descendants, 1952.

# For Further Information

## In the U.S.

Aptucxet Trading Post Museum, Box 95, Bourne, MA 02532-0795

Plimoth Plantation, P.O. Box 1620, Plymouth, MA 02360

## In the U.K.

Bassetlaw Museum, Amcott House, 40 Grove Street, Retford, Notts, DN22 6JU

# About the Author

Photo by Richard D. Foley

Sheila Foley is a teacher, author and artist. Her interest in history, particulary British history, usually prompts her to write historical fiction. *Faith Unfurled: The Pilgrims' Quest for Freedom,* is her first non-fiction book.

As an artist, Foley has illustrated the picture-book biography, *Leonard Bernstein: America's Maestro,* also from Discovery Enterprises, Ltd. But she is perhaps best known for the work she's done for her hometown of Stoneham, Massachusetts. Eight of Foley's paintings hang in public buildings there, including her favorite and most recent acrylic of Olympic skater Nancy Kerrigan.

# Other books in the
## *Perspectives on History Series:*

The Lowell Mill Girls: Life in the Factory
ISBN 1-878668-06-4

Voices from the West: Life Along the Trail
ISBN 1-878668-18-8

Coming to America: A New Life in a New Land
ISBN 1-878668-23-4

The New England Transcendentalists:
Life of the Mind and of the Spirit
ISBN 1-878668-22-6

Forward into Light: The Struggle for Women's Suffrage
ISBN 1-878668-25-0

The Cherokee Nation: Life Before the Tears
ISBN 1-878668-26-9

The Underground Railroad:
Life On the Road to Freedom
ISBN 1-878668-27-7

Each book in this series is $4.95.

To order these titles, please fill out the order form on the back and mail to Discovery Enterprises, Ltd. 134 Middle St., Suite 210, Lowell, MA 01852 or call 800-729-1720 to charge on (MC/VISA) M-F 8AM-5PM. You may also fax your orders 24 hrs. daily to 508-937-5779 (please include purchase order number.)

# Order Form

Ship to:

Name: _____

Address: _____

City: _____ State: _____ Zip: _____

Phone: _____ P.O. Number (if applicable): _____

| ISBN (last 3 digits) | Title | Qty | Total |
|---|---|---|---|
| | | | |
| | | | |
| | | | |
| | | | |
| | | | |
| | | | |
| | | Sub Total | |
| | | Shipping/Handling | |
| | | Total | |

Please add $1.50 per book shipping/handling or $5.00 for any orders over $19.00.